Machines at Work

Machines on the Farm

Siân Smith

Raintree

Raintree is an imprint of Capstone Global Library Limited, a company incorporated in England and Wales having its registered office at 7 Pilgrim Street, London, EC4V 6LB – Registered company number: 6695582

www.raintreepublishers.co.uk
myorders@raintreepublishers.co.uk

Text © Capstone Global Library Limited 2014
First published in hardback in 2014
Paperback edition first published in 2015
The moral rights of the proprietor have been asserted.

Edited by Dan Nunn and John-Paul Wilkins
Designed by Cynthia Akiyoshi
Picture research by Elizabeth Alexander
Production by Helen McCreath
Originated by Capstone Global Library Ltd
Printed and bound in China by Leo Paper Products Ltd

ISBN 978 1 406 25938 4 (hardback)
17 16 15 14 13
10 9 8 7 6 5 4 3 2 1

ISBN 978 1 406 25943 8 (paperback)
18 17 16 15 14
10 9 8 7 6 5 4 3 2 1

British Library Cataloguing in Publication Data
Smith, Siân.
Machines on the farm. – (Machines at work)
631.3-dc23
A full catalogue record for this book is available from the British Library.

Acknowledgements
We would like to thank the following for permission to reproduce photographs: Alamy pp. 8 (© David R. Frazier Photolibrary, Inc.), 14 (© AgStock Images, Inc.), 18, 23 milker (© Andrew Fox), 20 (© Joerg Boethling); Corbis 5 (© Juice Images), 15 (© Westend61); Getty Images pp. 4 (Darrell Gulin/Stockbyte), 9 (Bloomberg), 16 (Alvis Upitis/Stockbyte); Robert Harding p. title page (Emilio Ferrer/age footstock); Shutterstock pp. 6 (© Orientaly), 7 (© V. J. Matthew), 10 (© Deyan Georgiev), 12, 23 harvest (© Jose Ignacio Soto), 13, 23 bale (© Rihardzz), 19 (© chinahbzyg), 21 (© spflaum), 23 grain (© IDAL), 23 rows (© Straight 8 Photography); SuperStock pp. 11, 23 pesticides (© imagebroker.net), 17 (© Tips Images), 22 (© The Irish Image Collection).

Design element photographs of car engine part (© fuyu liu), gear cog (© Leremy), grain field (© haraldmuc), and wheat field (© oriontrail) reproduced with permission of Shutterstock.

Front cover photograph of reaping machine in a wheat field reproduced with permission of Robert Harding (Emilio Ferrer/age footstock). Back cover photograph of tractor (© Orientaly) and baler (© Rihardzz) reproduced with permission of Shutterstock.

We would like to thank Paul Charvill, Veronica Kitson, Dee Reid, and Marla Conn for their invaluable help in the preparation of this book.

Contents

Some words are shown in bold, **like this**. You can find out what they mean by looking in the glossary.

Why do we have machines on a farm?

A farm is a place where animals are kept or plants are grown.

Farmers sell the plants and animals for people to eat.

planter

Planters plant young plants in the ground.
Planting machines allow farmers to plant
many seeds or plants at a time.

How do machines help us to grow plants?

Farm machines can be used to water plants.

Sometimes the water can be controlled by clocks called timers.

helicopter

Some machines spray **pesticides**, to kill insects that eat plants.

On some big farms, helicopters are used to spray pesticides.

11

Which machines help to harvest plants?

Combine harvesters help farmers to **harvest** or pick **grain** plants.

They cut the plants and collect the seeds. Then they take the seeds out of their cases, and leave the straw behind.

bale

baler machine

Other machines take the straw, or hay from cut grass, and make it into **bales**.

They roll or squash it into round or square bales and tie it up.

Do all harvesting machines look the same?

Harvesting machines that pick and sort different types of plants can look very different.

Some large machines can be used to pick and sort tomatoes.

Grape picking machines have a large gap in the middle so that they can drive along **rows** of grape vines.

The machine shakes the grape vines and collects the grapes that fall down.

Some machines **harvest** vegetables that grow under the ground.

They pull the vegetables out or dig them up. The vegetables move along a belt and the machine gets rid of the soil.

potatoes

belt

16

Some machines collect fruit that grows on trees.

Olive harvesters shake the trees and catch the fruit that falls off.

Which farm machine milks cows?

Farmers use a **milker** to milk cows.

The farmer puts a milker onto each cow's four teats.

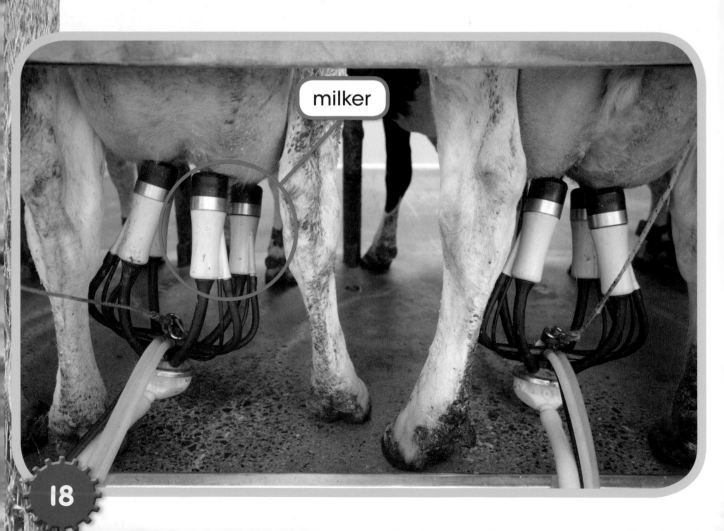

milker

When the machine starts, the milkers suck out milk. Pipes take the milk into large tanks to keep it cool.

When there is no more milk, the milkers drop off.

What other machines are used on a farm?

Farmers use other machines to help with many different jobs.

Tree cutters and other machines are used to keep farms safe and tidy.

Machines are used to sort or pack food items.

An egg sorter puts small, medium, and large eggs into boxes. The farmer can sell the different eggs at different prices.

What does this machine do?

Can you guess what this machine does?
Find the answer on page 24.

Picture glossary

bale hay or straw tied together in a bundle

grain seeds and cereals that come from grasses, including corn, wheat, and rice

harvest pick or collect

milker part of a machine used to milk cows. A milker sucks out milk from a cow's teats.

pesticides special liquids that are used on plants to kill insects

rows lines of things such as plants

Find out more

Books

Farm Machines (World of Farming), Nancy Dickmann (Raintree, 2011)

Tractors and Farm Vehicles (Mighty Machines), Jean Coppendale (QED Publishing, 2008)

Websites

www.deere.com/wps/dcom/en_US/corporate/ our_company/fans_visitors/kids/kids.page?
Play games and watch videos of farm machines.

www.kidcyber.com.au/topics/farms.htm
Learn more about what you might find on a farm.

Index

The farm machine on page 22 is spreading manure to help plants grow. Manure is made from animal waste.